Wild Animal Kingdom

BLACK BEARS

GAIL TERP

BLACK RABBIT BOOKS

Bolt is published by Black Rabbit Books
P.O. Box 3263, Mankato, Minnesota, 56002.
www.blackrabbitbooks.com
Copyright © 2017 Black Rabbit Books

Design and Production by Michael Sellner
Photo Research by Rhonda Milbrett

Library of Congress Control Number: 2015954865

HC ISBN: 978-1-68072-050-1   PB ISBN: 978-1-68072-307-6

Printed in the United States at CG Book Printers,
North Mankato, Minnesota, 56003. PO #1798 4/16

Web addresses included in this book were working and appropriate at the time of publication. The publisher is not responsible for broken or changed links.

Image Credits
Corbis: John Foster/Masterfile, 9
(tr); Michael Jones/Design Pics, 9 (br);
John E Marriott/All Canada Photos, 8–9;
Suzi Eszterhas/Minden Pictures, 18; James Hager, 24 (top); Getty: Daisy Gilardini, 11; Stephen Harrington, 12–13; Gail Shotlander, 17; Gerry Ellis, 26–27; istock: andyKRAKOVSKI, 32; bojanjanjic, 4–5; Dieter Meyrl, 3; Frank Leung, 21; jcrader, 6; jonmccormackphoto, 24 (bottom); RyersonClark, 8 (tl); National Geographic Creative: PAUL NICKLEN, Cover; Shutterstock: Abbie, 31; Andrea Izzotti, 6–7; Denis Tabler, 22–23; DoubleBubble, Back Cover, 1, 14–15 (background); Nebojsa S, 14, 18–19 (silhouette bears); Tory Kallman, 28; Wikimedia: 14–15 (map)
Every effort has been made to contact copyright holders for material reproduced in this book. Any omissions will be rectified in subsequent printings if notice is given to the publisher.

Contents

CHAPTER 1

A Day in the  Life

It's a day in late fall. A black bear sniffs the air. It smells acorns. The nuts are one of its favorite foods. Shuffling to a spot near a tree, the bear digs. Up in the tree, a squirrel chatters. The bear finds the squirrel's buried acorns. The squirrel is not pleased, but the bear is.

How Big Is a Black Bear?

SHOULDER HEIGHT
2 TO 3 FEET
(.6 to .9 meters)

A Smell in the Air

The bear eats all the acorns in the hole. It points its nose up and sniffs again. There are more acorns, but they're not close by. It walks toward the smell.

The bear walks for an hour. It comes to a large group of trees full of acorns. For five days, it climbs trees and crams itself with food. When full, it leaves the trees a much fatter bear.

LENGTH
4 TO 7 FEET
(1 to 2 meters)

300 375 450
225 525
150 600
75 675
0 750
pounds   pounds

WEIGHT
200 TO 500 POUNDS
(91 to 227 kilograms)

By the Numbers

880
POUNDS · · · · ·
(399 kg)
TOP WEIGHT

42
TEETH

35
MILES
(56 KILOMETERS)
PER HOUR

TOP RUNNING SPEED

3 TO 6 INCHES
(8 TO 15 cm)

TAIL LENGTH

UP TO 5 MILES
(8 KM)

SWIMMING DISTANCE

UP TO 15 SQUARE MILES
(39 square km)

A FEMALE'S HOME RANGE

10 to 15 YEARS LIFE SPAN

CHAPTER 2

Food to Eat

and a Place to Live

Black bears eat both plants and animals. Most of their **diet** is made up of plants. In spring, they eat grass, flowers, and roots. They munch berries in summer. In fall, they enjoy acorns and other nuts.

Black bears eat meat in spring, summer, and fall. They eat the **young** of large animals, such as deer. They eat insects, fish, and mice too.

Home Sweet Home

The big diet of black bears helps them live in many **habitats**. Some live in forests. Others live in mountains or swamps. Wherever they live, bears must be able to find lots of food. And they must have spots where they can hide from **predators**.

Black bears love to snack on ants. They use their claws to rip open rotting logs. Then they slurp up the ants with their sticky tongues.

Black Bear Range Map

CHAPTER 3

Family Life

In winter, there is little food for black bears. So all summer and fall they eat lots of food. In late fall, each bear finds a den. A den might be a **hollow** log. It could be a space under a large rock. The bears **hibernate** in their dens all winter. They don't eat or drink.

COMPARING SIZES

Cubs Are Born

Partway through winter, female bears give birth. Each female has up to three cubs. To keep warm, the cubs snuggle with their mothers.

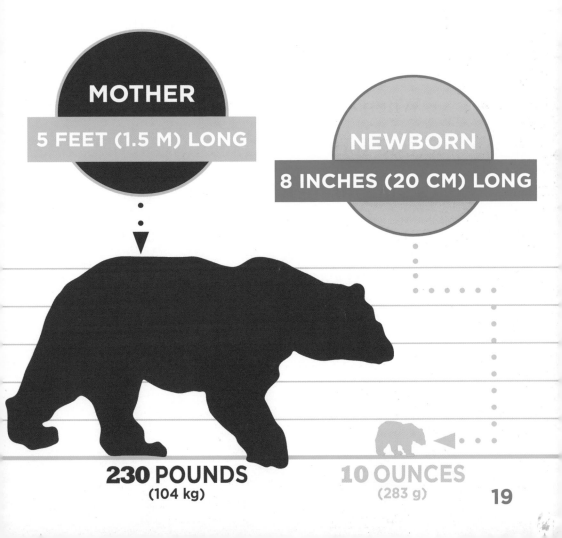

MOTHER

5 FEET (1.5 M) LONG

NEWBORN

8 INCHES (20 CM) LONG

230 POUNDS
(104 kg)

10 OUNCES
(283 g)

Learning to Survive

In spring, the bears leave their dens. Cubs stay close to their mothers. They must learn what foods to eat. They also have to learn what dangers to avoid. In fall, they hibernate with their mothers one more time.

When cubs leave their dens the second spring, they are one year old. It's time for them to go out on their own. Each cub has to find its own food. And each must find its own place to live.

BLACK BEAR FEATURES

EARS WITH GREAT HEARING

NOSE WITH A STRONG SENSE OF SMELL

LONG STICKY TONGUE

SHORT TAIL

CURVED CLAWS

THICK FUR

Crazy Colors

Not all black bears are black. Some are brown or reddish-brown. The Kermode bear of Canada is white.

CHAPTER 4

Predators

and Other Threats

Adult black bears have few predators. But grizzly bears, foxes, and eagles **prey** on cubs. Mother bears watch for danger. If they see trouble, they send their cubs up trees. The cubs are safe there.

Human Threat

Humans are black bears' main **threat**. Some people hunt bears. Others build homes and stores on bear habitats. These buildings take away land bears live on.

Laws now limit when bears can be hunted. Lawmakers have also protected land for bears. People can't hunt or build on those lands.

Protecting Black Bears

Long ago, black bears lived all across the United States. Today, only about 750,000 black bears live in North America. People have learned a lot about these smart animals. But there is still work to do to protect the bears' homes.

diet (DY-uht)—food and drink that an animal eats

habitat (HAB-uh-tat)—the place where a plant or animal grows or lives

hibernate (HI-bur-nayt)—to pass the winter in a sleeping or resting state

hollow (HAWL-oh)—an unfilled space

predator (PRED-uh-tuhr)—an animal that eats other animals

prey (PRAY)—to catch and eat something

threat (THRET)—something that can do harm

young (YUNG)—animals that are recently born or hatched

BOOKS

Borgert-Spaniol, Megan. *Black Bears.* North American Animals. Minneapolis: Bellwether Media, 2015.

Graubart, Norman D. *How to Track a Black Bear.* Scatalog: Kid's Field Guide to Animal Poop. New York: Windmill Books, 2015.

Magby, Meryl. *Black Bears.* American Animals. New York: PowerKids Press, 2014.

WEBSITES

American Black Bear
www.biokids.umich.edu/critters/ Ursus_americanus/

American Black Bear Facts for Kids
naturemappingfoundation.org/natmap/facts/ american_black_bear_kle.htm

Black Bear Facts
www.ngkids.co.uk/did-you-know/Black-bear-facts